HORSE INDIAN WOLF

In appreciation of all wild animals.
Each life is precious and important.

In honor of Native Americans.
Their bond with nature and wild things
should be treasured and emulated.

With gratitude to my beloved family
and friends, who are always supporting,
always inspiring.

J. P. L.

Celebrating all artists who keep wildlife
and wild lands alive in song and story,
paint and poetry, film and photography.
Thank you.

K. V. K.

A GREENWICH WORKSHOP PRESS BOOK
©2010 The Greenwich Workshop Press
All paintings ©2010 Judy Larson®

ISBN–13: 978-086713-150-5

Published by The Greenwich Workshop, Inc.
151 Main St., Seymour, CT 06483
(800) 243-4246

Library of Congress Cataloging-in-Publication Data
is available upon request.

The art of Judy Larson® is published in fine art limited editions by The Greenwich Workshop, Inc. Visit our website to find one of our Authorized Dealers: *www.greenwichworkshop.com*.

Illustration credits
©iStockphoto.com and Peter Zelei: antique paper texture throughout; Luseen Leiber: feathers pp. 1, 14, 20, 26, 41 (left feather), 47; Laurence Dean: trees pp. 5, 31, 33, bears pp. 11, 13; Pavel Losevsky: wolves pp. 5 (bottom left and upper right), 6, 8 (upper left and lower left), 31, 37; 4x6: wolves on jacket, pp. 5 (upper left), 28; John Spencer: children p. 7; A-Digit: wolves pp. 8 (right side), 39, birds p.18, 48 rider p. 25; Diane Labombarbe: branches pp. 10, 25, 31, 36, 39, 40, 41; ©creating-more: paws pp. 11, 32, 33; ziggymaj: buffalo p. 14 and jacket; Helga Jaunegg: horses pp. 17, 18, 22, 42; Kate Leigh: rider p. 19; Gary Hudson: feathers pp. 22, 41 (right feather); tanteckken: birds pp. 23, 34 (bottom), and jacket; Ceren Evin Erkan: mountains p. 42; oblachko: bird p. 34 (top); Brandon Laufenberg: rifle p. 25. ©Thinkstock: Indian silo pp. 17, 20. ©Bigstock and Inna Esina: tipi pp. 22, 36.

Jacket front: *In Spirit Only* (detail)
Jacket back: *The Pursued*

Design: Bjorn Akselsen
Manufactured in Singapore by CS Graphics
First printing 2010
1 2 3 4   13 12 11 10

HORSE
INDIAN
WOLF

The Hidden Pictures of JUDY LARSON *by* KATHLEEN V. KUDLINSKI

NINE TO FIVE

Stories and secrets surround us.
Native People read them on Mother Earth's face.
Horses, Indians, and Wolves
could teach us to see again.

Turn back a page. Look again. You saw it, didn't you?
The horses sense an eagle overhead.
Their skins shudder as its shadow passes.
They feel its spirit still, on their skins, in their hearts.

Here, five People travel an ancient path.
They know they share Mother Earth with others.
Can you see their story?
The horses sense danger.
Heads high, eyes wide, they snort and prance.
The riders feel their fear. They read the woodland signs.
Who passed here?
Nine wolves have left their mark.
Tracks. Fur tufts. Sharp scents and dog-like droppings.
The People feel the spirits of their Brother Wolves.
Do you see the wolf pack? Look again.

Wolf cubs play free in sunshine.
They roughhouse and wrestle and learn of their strength.
They see the wild birds and learn all their calls.
They smell the fresh wind and learn of its scents.
When they feel hunger, the pack will provide.
Food comes, and they learn the flavors;
rabbit and quail, deer, bison, and squirrel.
Soon they will learn to hunt.

Native children play under the same sun.
When they feel hunger, their tribe will provide.
Rabbit and quail, deer, bison, and squirrel,
fish and antelope, nuts, fruits, and honey.
Soon they will learn to hunt and to cook.
Outdoors, these children learn their strength.
They learn the birds and the breezes.
They study wild animals and learn their ways.
Sometimes, sometimes, they play with wolf cubs.
This they remember forever. So do the wolves.
Once, two children were here with these wolf cubs.
Do you see their spirits?
Look again.

Judy Larson ©1998

Child's Play

INTENT

Black wolf seems shy. She is not.
She sits atop the food chain and more.
She is Alpha, winner of she-wolf contests.
Her mate is Alpha Male, strongest he-wolf.
Only the Alpha Pair can raise pups.
Their babies have grown this summer.
She thinks of two puppies.
They are hungry at home.
Can you see them?

BROTHERS AND SISTERS

Wintertime.
Past year's pups have grown big,
yet they stay, all but one.
One white wolf wandered off
to start a new pack.
His spirit stays, proud in their memory.
Can you see him?
This pack grows hungry and all must be fed:
Alpha parents, their children,
and new babies, too.
They howl and meet, hunt and eat,
then play and sleep together.

THE FAMILY TREE

Brave Brother Bear is striding alone,
secure in his strength and his size.
He eats like The People—
meats, greens, fruits and findings.
Few challenge his might
or his right.

But Brother Bear watches for one fiercer still.
Mother Bear.

Three cubs in tow, she wanders the woods.
Do you see them? Look again.
No pack, herd or tribe will help raise these young.
Mother must manage alone.

Gentle in nurture when teaching her cubs,
Fearsome in battle to save their young lives,
Mother lives beyond brave.
She fights to the death to save her wee cubs
and the future of bears
everywhere.

SPIRITS OF GRIZZLY CREEK

Dark woods hold danger.
Swift waters mask risks.
Fear readies its attack.

The People hunger for Brother Bear's nerve.
They wear his claws
and show off his sign,
to summon the strength of his Spirit.

This rider trusts his sure-footed mount
but calls Bear Spirits for comfort.
One towers to grant grizzly courage.
One runs within a frightened steed.

Do you see them? Look again.

AIR AND ESCAPE

Eyes widen, ears flicker —
the hunted fear hunters.
Fear keeps them alive.
Horse, pronghorn, and bison,
and hares, pack rats, and mice
who are low on the food chain.
Always at risk.

Nostrils flare.
Smell man, bear, wolf?   Run!
Sniff smoke, flood, fire?   Flee!
Scent mate, friend, foe?   Respond!
Sense water, shade, fresh grasses?
Relax.

Look here. Three bison sniff air,
two brown but one, white.
Do you see?
White bison, so rare and so sacred
that their death, horns, and skin
held great power for all.

HE DOG

The People could hunt the wild horses for food.
They didn't.
The People could tan the wild horse skins to wear.
They didn't.
The People could work captured horses as slaves.
They didn't.
Instead,
They called all wild horses the Earth's "Sacred Dogs"
and bonded in spirit with horses they rode.
No spurs and no bits, no cinch-saddles—just trust—
they galloped as one on The Plains in the past.

Look.
Look again.
See the face in his face?
This horse still remembers the rider he loved.
He Dog, a Crow Chief, a great horseman—right there.
Their two-headed spirit lives, caught in this art.

Spotted ponies ran wild.
Nez Perce tamed, trained, and traded them.
Quick-witted, sure-footed,
battle-brave, beautiful,
good medicine for warriors.
Three normal mounts fetched
One Appaloosa.

Crow People marked them with war symbols
To add courage, double strength, inspire terror.
These painted ponies
are far more than horses.

The People knew crow birds,
as smart, wise, and social.
Three crows grace these horses.
Did you see them? Look again.

CROW PONIES

Judy Larson ©1991

18

Ebenezer and the War Horse

Chief Joseph painted his black war horse.
Put paint on his racer, too.
No mount flew faster than Ebenezer.
Together they won every race.
But Chief Joseph lost the last battle
and rode the dark horse to his surrender.
Look there. He's still racing on Ebenezer's neck.
It's our wins we will want well remembered.

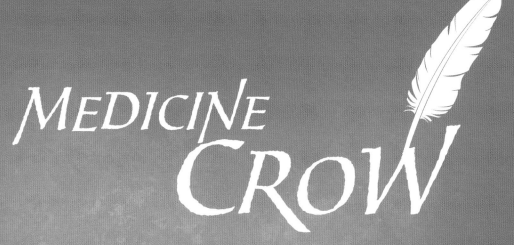

MEDICINE CROW

Crow People were wise.
They chose brave over brutal.
Chief Medicine Crow
fought close-in to touch his foes.
He counted courage by coups, not kills,
taking only lives truly threatening
his children, clan, family, or tribe.

Do you see the Chief here,
come to count your coup?
Look again.

Medicine Crow put no paint on this pony,
fastened in feathers to flutter, instead.
Red-tailed Hawk feathers.
The warrior's headdress bore a whole hawk,
so horse, man, and hawk
flew to battle as one, swift and fierce and fearless.

Judy Larson
©2000

Judy Larson © 2008

THE HORSE TIPI

Blackfeet elders told tribal truths through stories.
They said: There was a man whose horse lay injured.
He camped by his side as the battle moved on.
He dabbed yellow paint on the worst of the wounds.
He smudged scented grass in the air all around.
He stayed and he sang the horse old sacred songs.
Three times his stallion faltered; the fourth, he stood.
The man led him home, and his thanks waited there:
A horse-painted tipi and the gift now to heal.

Look. Do you see the man riding free?

THE CROW TIPI

There was a man, a Blackfeet of fame,
who shared all he stole on his raids.
His jealous chief cursed him with native witchcraft.
Three times the man rode out to battle for his tribe.
Three times his horses abandoned him, running away.
He trudged all night long on dark plains to get home.
Dream spirit came. Spoke.
"You shared bison meat with my children, the crows.
You give when unasked.
A crow-painted tipi is yours, in thanks.
And you have the right to be chief."

Look. Do you see the mark of the crow on the horse?

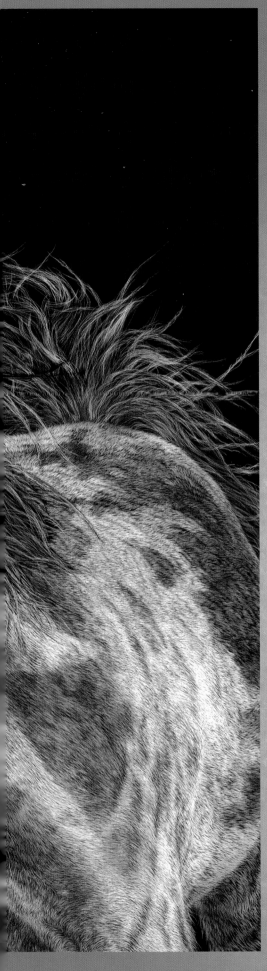

THE RESISTERS

For years and years they roamed the wild West
In balance with nature and honoring life.
In nineteen and nineteen,
the Crow heard the worst.
"All our cities need beef and the wild plains are plowed.
All your land now must pasture our cattle.
Kill. Kill your wild horses—or we will."
"No," said the Crow. "Kill our Brothers?"
No.
"You had your chance," came the answer.
A four-dollar bounty helped Whites do the deed,
paying cowboys and hired hands alike.
They killed the wild herds and the Native's stock, too.
By nineteen and thirty all sacred dogs died,
forty thousand head gone without honor.
The Crow way of life,
Gone.

Look. Two bounty hunters ride
without honor.
Two horses run for their lives.

Chief Red Horse, Lakota, lived past the day
of the Battle of Little Bighorn.
He scattered, regrouped, and in the next years,
Remembering,
sketched war scenes in bold color
for the future.

RED HORSE

He drew Company E, each on a pale gray.
Outnumbered by Natives, they had to give way.
The Whites lost that battle.
Some horses got free.
They scattered and were captured by Natives.
For years these horses, remembering,
birthed new foals of warm gray
for the future.

When you find Red Horse in the painting,
Remember.

FLIGHT

The People were few.
They took from the Earth
what they needed,
no more.
White settlers came.
There were many, then came vast numbers more.
Now we take what we will, what we need, what we want
with our guns, and with poisons, for food, bounty, sport,
from four-wheeled truck, snow sled, and winged plane.
We level the forest and till up the land.
We've broken the balance,
and Mother Earth cries.
A few people hear.

Look.
Horses wheel, a wolf runs in terror.
Is a hunter's plane droning overhead?

THE VANISHING

So many gone:
Horses, and Indians, and wolves.
What is done cannot be changed.
We honor them now
in our paintings and songs
and in stories and films and dance.

Here, three Spirit horses
hold three Spirit wolves.
Look long, give them honor again.
Pause. Listen. Think.
What we do can be swayed.
Let truth rise fierce inside you.
Sing. Paint. Dance.
Make new films, books, and poems
for minds yet to come.
The future
is unfinished
art.

Judy Larson © 2003

THE PURSUED

Natives speak of Wolf Medicine.
Look a wolf in the eye.
It does not flinch, but gazes at you
as an equal on Earth.

Natives knew the wolves, calling them
Great Hunter,
for wolves provide for all,
the pups, the old, and the sick.
Great Teacher,
for wolves bring the young new skills,
new ideas, and new pathways.
Great Protector,
for wolves defend their territory,
their pack, and themselves, and
Great Spirit,
for wolves live lightly,
in balance with Earth and all others.

And yet wolves look at you as an equal.
Are you?
It makes you think
about what they are. What you could be.
Wolf Medicine begins.

Do you see yet a fourth wolf? He is looking at you.

Paws and Reflect

Eagle lost a feather.
Flew after it in play.
Soared and spiraled and swooped with it,
rested his weary wings
and sighed.

Native caught the feather
Tied red leather strips on it.
Danced and sang and dangled it,
rested his heavy head
and smiled.

Cougar caught the feather,
lay in sunny warmth to play.
Batted, bit, and bullied it,
rested her large paws
and purred.

Look. Do you see them?
Nine eagles watch the feather's fate.

THE SURVIVORS

Nature brings disasters:
earthquakes, aftershocks, and tidal waves,
hurricanes, tornados, floods, forest fires.
Life is fierce. It survives.
Look. Here, after fire, in the grasses' new greening.
The mewling of calf can be heard.
Life survives.

Man makes more disasters:
Clear-cut woods, oil spills, greenhouse skies,
mining pits, acid seas, and genocides.
Life is fierce. It survives.
Or it tries—it needs our help.
Look here, after man killed most
of the wild bison, they now thrive again on our land.
With our care, life survives.

Look again.
A Native in buffalo headdress, awaits your answer.
Do you care?

A TIME TO HEAL

The Nez Perce life was horses
and their Spirit-filled land.
The government knew.
To kill tribal spirit, they fought the Nez Perce,
killed their Appaloosas, and all the nearby wolves.
Their spirit flickered.
Then,
From less than three hundred Appys, there are thousands now.
From a small shadow tribe, Nez Perce came blazing back.
To help with their healing, they took in a wolf pack
to show all the world how fierce Spirit can be.

Look. Chief Joseph and a wolf hide in this painting.

THREE WOLVES

Mexican wolves roamed the deep, dry Southwest.
They'd been there forever. Ranchers killed them, all.
Some people cared.
They brought a few wolves from the south of the border.
Look here. Now a new pack runs free, joyfully wild.

And see who runs alongside!

A tiny herd of Mustangs hid out three hundred years
in the San Luis Mountains, alone. Drought threatened them all.
Some people cared.
They brought all the horses to breeders and ranches.
Look here. Now new foals run wild, joyfully safe.

Judy Larson ©2000

KINSHIP

Alpha pair runs together,
and other wolves join in.
The pack follows nearby.
They chase one goal together:
keeping wolfkind strong on Earth.

Look—
A Native couple works together
and another friend joins in.
The tribe follows nearby.
They chase many goals together,
pooling energies toward great works.

Children and wolf pups run with their kin
taught by tribe or by wise pack elders.
Then they learn even more from
Great Mother Earth
in play and discovery outdoors.
Stories and secrets wait there for you, too.
Look—do you see them?
Go outside. Look again.

PRYOR COMMITMENT

They look to us now. There is no one else
to save horse, grizzly, bison, and wolf.
We let them down once, dishonoring Earth.

For five hundred years these mustangs survived
from stock that came over from Spain.
Again ranchers wanted the land where they ranged.
"No, wait," people said, and they fought for the mustangs.
They preserved Pryor Mountains and left them untamed
to be home to wild horses forever.
Look. Do you see little foals?
They play on the mountain today.

But what of all the others, with whom we share the Earth,
grizzlies, cougars, bison, wild horses, wolves, and more?
If we work together
we can save them all.

KEY TO HIDDEN PICTURES

NINE TO FIVE   4

CHILD'S PLAY   6/7

INTENT   9

BROTHERS AND SISTERS   9

THE FAMILY TREE   10/11

SPIRITS OF GRIZZLY CREEK   12/13

AIR AND ESCAPE 15

HE DOG 16

CROW PONIES 18

EBENEZER AND THE WAR HORSE 19

MEDICINE CROW 21

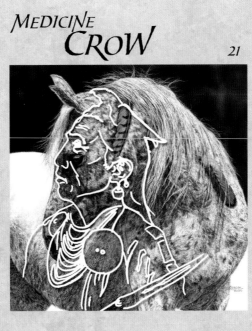

THE HORSE TIPI 22

THE CROW TIPI 23

THE RESISTERS 24/25

RED HORSE 26/27

45

FLIGHT

28/29

THE VANISHING

30

THE PURSUED

32/33

PAWS AND REFLECT

34/35

THE SURVIVORS

37

A TIME TO HEAL

38

THREE WOLVES

39

KINSHIP

40/41

PRYOR COMMITMENT

43

ABOUT THE ARTWORK

Each of Judy Larson's paintings takes months to complete. First, she makes many sketches to work out her composition, carefully including the hidden elements that will help to tell the story of the painting. She transfers the outlines of the animals from her drawing to a Claybord,™ a hardboard covered with a velvet-smooth, solid coating of white clay ground. Then, Judy paints black India ink all over each animal's silhouette. When the ink is dry, she transfers the details of her pencil drawing onto this black silhouette. She uses hundreds of fine X-Acto® knife blades to scratch thousands of lines through the black ink to show the white clay surface below. Each fine, thin scratch becomes a hair or fur. Long before finishing the black and white drawing, though, Judy paints each animal's moist, expression-filled eyes, distinctive mouth, and wet nose with acrylic paints. When they look real and lifelike, she completes the scratchboard part of her art. Next, she airbrushes colorful, transparent acrylic inks over each animal, tinting the exposed white clay. Backgrounds are airbrushed or painted with acrylic paint. Judy's last step is scratching through ink and color to bring out highlights, create whiskers, and other small details. Finally, she sprays the board with a sealer to make the artwork permanent.

To see a work in process and to learn more about Judy, go to *www.judylarson.com*. Any aspiring artist can try the very basics of Judy's technique with pre-inked Scratchbord™ and an X-Acto® knife, available at many art supply stores and through the Internet.

For younger artists, a beautiful scratchboard effect can be created with crayons. First, use brightly-colored crayons to cover regular paper in a pattern of rainbows, stripes, or scribbles. Next, use a black crayon to cover over the bright colors. Finally, using the tines of a fork, the end of a paper clip, the tip of a toothpick, or any stiff pointed object, scratch through the black to show the glowing colors beneath.

LEARN MORE

HORSES

Appaloosa Horse Club Learn all about the breed today and its history, register your horse, visit the online Appaloosa Museum, and more. *www.appaloosa.com*

National Wild Horse and Burro Program at the U. S. Department of the Interior, Bureau of Land Management Learn what is being done to protect and manage wild herds and how you could adopt a captured wild horse or burro. *www.blm.gov/wo/st/en/prog/wild_horse_and_burro.html*
www.blm.gov/mt/st/en/fo/billings_field_office/wildhorses.html

The Cloud Foundation This non-profit organization is dedicated to the protection and preservation of wild horses and burros on our western public lands, particularly a herd in the Arrowhead Mountains of Montana. *www.thecloudfoundation.org*

INDIANS

Smithsonian Institute Archives Search for Red Horse's pictographs of The Battle at Little Bighorn, archived at several locations in this extensive site. *www.siarchives.si.edu*

Nez Perce Tribal Web Site Learn about the organization and activities of the Nez Perce Tribe today and interesting facts about their way of life throughout history. *www.nezperce.org*

Official Site of the Crow Tribe Learn about the current affairs of the Crow Tribe as well as their history, and view extensive photo-archives. *www.crowtribe.com*

Blackfeet Nation Visit this site for a clear explanation of Blackfeet culture and current affairs plus a wonderful collection of ancient Blackfeet stories. *www.blackfeetnation.com*

WOLVES

Defenders of Wildlife Learn more about wolves, the threats they face today and what you can do to help. *www.defenders.org/wildlife_and_habitat/wildlife/wolf,_gray.php*

National Wildlife Foundation This organization leads the fight to save many kinds of wildlife and habitats. Look up wolves and bison, eagles, and wild horses for news about their survival. Includes actions you can take to help. *www.nwf.org*

The Wolf Education and Research Center The Center provides a home for a pack of wolves on Nez Perce land and operates under the tribe's supervision. *www.wolfcenter.org*

The International Wolf Center Dedicated to advancing the survival of wolves, this center teaches about wolves and their relationship to wild lands and the human role in their future. This center even has web cams where you might catch a live peek at a wolf in Ely, Minnesota. *www.wolf.org*